# WHERE THE
# HEART FEELS SAFE

KIMBERLY ZIEGLER BASHAM

# WHERE THE HEART FEELS SAFE

*First, I want to thank God for giving me the talent to write.*

*Next, I want to thank James and Jami for their
unwavering love and support.*

*Then, I want to thank my family and friends
for the encouragement.*

*Finally, I want to remember my womb-mate, Tim,
who would be cheering me on.*

# Table of Contents

# 1

## *Where the Heart Feels Safe*

The best of friends is not easy to find
But the bond they share endures the test of time.

The best of friends takes no effort to keep
But they are there to laugh when you are happy,
cry when you weep.

The best of friends is what I found in you
Yes, I consider you to be most faithful and true.

The best of friends ground you as a rock
Even when your time has ended its earthly clock.

The best of friends are blessings to embrace
Because they are where your heart feels safe.

2

# Jesus-colored Glasses

He looks on me with Jesus-colored glasses.
    My sins are covered beneath my Savior's blood.
He looks on me with Jesus-colored glasses.
And sees me as His perfect child.

# Ways of the World

I can't change the ways of the world,
    and make it a safe place for the young boys and girls.
I can't change the minds of stubborn men -
to open their eyes to see my Savior and Friend.

# 3

## *Blush*

Lord, forgive me for I have forgotten how to blush.
My eyes have seen many horrors and, for You,
my lips have stayed in a hush.
My heart once was open and tender –
longing to hear Your name.
But my mind became a playground where the
demons play out Satan's evil game.
Slowly, but very surely, I grow colder day by day.
Replacing the truth of Your Word with what
those of this cruel world do say.
Lord, I pray You will break through the layers
of stone in my heart.
Shatter it, Lord, and sculpt it into a magnificent piece of art.
Solely for Your pleasure – no longer in my control.
Only in You to find delight –
dead to the evils lurking in the night.

# 4

## *Revealed*

T hat my flaws and imperfections are forever sealed.
Sanctified and set apart, Your Word revealed.

## *There for You*

I f you're feeling like you're drowning in your problems,
the Lord is there for you.
If you're feeling like the mad rush of this world is
sweeping you away and out of control,
the Lord is there for you.
If you're feeling like the temptations of sin are
weakening your walk,
the Lord is there for you.
Turn to the Lord with all your concerns and worry,
for He alone has the power to help you.
Remember always, the battle is over,
and the victory has already been won!

# 5

## *Lost in the Mire*

Today, I did it again.
I turned from You and jumped into a cesspool of sin.

Covered in filth from my head to my toes,
My attitude was flippant – that's right, anything goes.

But deep down inside under my false smiling grin,
My heart felt queasy and wanted to give in.

To give up the rouse and turn back around
Scared You'd be gone and no longer to be found.

I was lost in the mire and sinking so fast.
Finally, my heart betrayed me to the fullest.

And when I felt I was breathing my last,
Your Spirit startled me, and I turned back in alarm.
Your hand reached out to me and removed me from harm.

# 6

## *My Lord*

J esus is Lord of everything.
  Yes, He controls it all.
He is the way, and He is the key.
By His command, we shall fall down
on our knees and looking up into
His majestic face.  He'll make the
decision of eternity all based upon
a simple word so often skipped right on by.
It's not just that He is Lord –
it's whether we say, "My."

## *Blanket of Calm*

T he snow falls like a blanket of calm and quiet.
  The delicate flakes build up masses of
beautiful trees and covered paths.
The cold of the outside is reflected in
icy windows and frosty doors.
But the snow falls still like a soothing song –
Reminding us of the comforts of being home.

# 7

## *Invited Him In*

My sins have been forgiven by the grace He imparts.
    My life has been changed forever,
and we shall never be apart.
He'll walk with me always for I've invited Him in.
He'll even carry me if I cannot lift up my burdens.
My joys shall be many and my sorrows will be few.
For I have accepted Jesus and can no longer be lost –
this is true..

## *Shadow of the Cross*

Living in the shadow of the Cross.
    Heartbroken and sorrows for the
many that would be lost.
Yet, my Savior said as down His burden He laid.
For even I was worth His all which was paid.

# 8

## *Liberty*

I started as a seed on a far and distant shore.
   A desire burning in a heart – desolate and poor.
A hunger and a thirst; a cry for justice and more.
I planted in the hearts of a few tender, brave men.
And kindled like a fire gently stoked by a fresh wind.
I grew into a thought pondered in pure minds.
And slowly into a movement that would
leave my shores behind.
I was tossed and beaten across the stormy sea.
I lost some whose hearts carried me and
whose tongues spread my name.
I landed in a new world destined to be free
But prices had to be paid before I knew true Liberty.

# 9

## *We'll Meet in Heaven*

I may never know you and our earthly paths
    may never meet, but I want to thank you
for spending more time on your knees than your feet.
How blessed I am to have a friend like you who doesn't
really know me but continues to pray on through.
Yes, a golden prayer warrior sent here by my Lord –
To work quietly and long to increase the voices
singing that great Redemption song.
You may never know me, and you may not care.
But I saw you by God's vision and put you in my prayer.
You may never know me, and we may only meet by
the power of God's sweet grace –
bowing at the Savior's feet.
That you may never know me is a fact that I hold true.
But it will not stop the hope I hold that Jesus saves you too.
You may never know me, and for me, that is okay.
But if my prayer is answered, we'll meet in Heaven someday.
You may never know me, but by God's saving power,
Someday, you'll be given the vision of a helping
a needing stranger in their crucial hour.

# 10-11

## *On the Way*

I reach out my hands to touch you.
    I reach out my hands to laud you.
I reach out my hands to guide you on your way.
He reached out His hands to touch me.
He reached out His hands to hold me.
He reached out His hands to guide me on the way.
He is the Lord. He will love you.
He is the Lord. He will teach you.
He is the Lord. He will guide you on the way.

# This Man

This man's spirit walked with God
    Though on this earth his feet did trod.
This man's heart sought Heaven's reward
And by many he was loved and adored.
This man's life was fill with faith, hope, and love –
His earthly legacy exchanged for blessings above.
This man was husband, father, Pappy, and friend –
Humble, wise, endearing and kind.
This man shared Christ with all he embraced
And now, he has met Jesus face-to-face.

# 12

## *Our Cherished One*

Our hearts were filled with anticipation and joy.
    You were looking into our faces –
Our sweet baby boy.

Our lives were re-arranged with play dates and fun.
You were counting and reading and growing –
Our brown-eyed son.

Our days were strangely peaceful and a bit mundane.
You were becoming a graduate, husband, and father –
Our do-nut-making man.

Our eyes were overflowing with the rushing of tears.
You were no longer present in too short of years.
Our hearts were shattered and our lives have been changed.

You are in heaven –
Our cherished one.

## *The Story of Mildred*

Tell us the story of Mildred.
       Not just a poem or a song.
Tell us the story about her life.
Something with purpose and something true.

To keep her memory living in the hearts of those she knew.
Tell us about the day she was born in
a small Kentucky town.
Tell us of her sweet, soft scent swaddled in her gown.
Tell us about that toddling child with tussled hair
and mischievous smiles taking her first steps.

Tell us about her girlish squeals, her family, or her pets.
Tell us of those awkward years when
innocence begins to flee.
And through all the fuss and hurt and tears,

A young woman comes to be.
Tell us of her falling in love and taking someone's hand.
With intention and commitment symbolized
by her wedding band.

Tell us about her becoming a mom –
the awesomeness of that moment.

Of the confusion and fear and amazement
she felt with the birth of each of her children.
Tell us of her children – her daughter and her sons.
Each a testimony of her compassion and her love.

Tell us about her passion for her family and her friends.
Or of love for the Cats and of playing cards;
Of sewing and quilting and stitching in love;
Of cooking and praying and trusting God above.

Tell us of her growing old – of the silver in her hair
And of the grace that sparkled in her eyes.
Tell us of her losing strength and sharing her last goodbyes.

Tell us of that sweet, dear peace nestled in her soul –
Of when she gave her heart to Christ
And made heaven her eternal home.

Tell us how she now is whole – no more suffering or pain.
And that though faith in Jesus, we'll see her once again.

# *Christmas Winter Rose*

Mom is my Christmas angel though
    she has no halo or wings.
Her hair has turned gray and with her heart she now sings.
She has been through Spring, Summer and Fall.
Each season she embraced with wonder, joy, love and awe.
Now, she faces the fullness ow Winter's last stand.
She is not alone for I am holding her hand.
Her life has been enchanting –
intriguing to some, I suppose –
With the fragrant depth of beauty as a Winter Rose.

# I Believe in Him

Oh, what a beautiful day. Oh, what a glorious morning.
Never had I felt so loved.
Never had my troubles been so few.

Oh, what a burden was lifted. Oh, how the tears did fall.
Never had I felt so blessed.
Never would I have ever guessed.

That His love could touch a heart so cold.
That trusting in Him would destroy a wall so old.

Oh, what a mystery it is. Oh, what a treasure I have found.
Never could I have ever dreamed.
Never would I have believed.

Oh, what a price was paid. Oh, how His mercy did save.
Never did I ever deserve. Never could I ever repay.

That His grace could make me an heir.
That by faith in Him, my life was spared.

Oh, what a beautiful day it will be.
Oh, what a happy song I will sing.

Always to be with the saints of God.
Always to be with my Savior and King.

Oh, what a joy I will find there.
Oh, how wonderful it will feel.

Always walking the streets of gold.
Always knowing He kept His promise of old.

That He suffered, He died, and He rose again;
That eternal life was granted because I believe in Him.

# 18-19

## *The Day After Christmas*

The day after Christmas – what a let down.
A baby in a manger, no throne or crown.
Angels in glorious voice singing.
Wise men gold, frankincense, and myrrh did bring.
And as dawn breaks across the eastern sky,
No more is heard of the shepherd's glad cry.
For though Messiah was finally here,
Life went back to normal year after year.
The Babe, He grew day by day.
Until after thirty years, He began His way.
So long after that first Christmas night,
Messiah would now claim His awesome birthright.
But who would listen, who would care,
Who would realize this Light so rare.
Who born of a virgin, hand-picked by God.
In a stable where the lowly often did trod.
Soon, He would die, nailed to a cross.
That mankind's sin could not bring a loss.
For those who welcome Him in their hearts.
Forever to live and never departs.
For Christmas was our Savior born.

Long ago on that first Christmas morn.
And Christ died for us on a lonely tree.
That Easter could set each captive free.
So, when in the valley,
Where we live and pray.
We have the hope of the mountain top
On our earthly dying day.

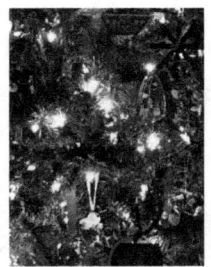

# *May I Have This Dance?*

L ife's dance is full of milestones.
    We treasure each and every on.
Often, it goes in circles,
and then you dip to have some fun.
Yes, life's dance is full of milestones –
many happy, many sad,
but for those who are truly blessed,
each milestone they are glad they had.
So, do not for me be sad now -
this I truly pray.
For the music does continue,
and I am dancing still today.

## 21

## *The Ties that Bind*

The ties that bind are not worn with suits.
  They are woven through life with courage and strength.
They are decorated with memories and truth.
The ties that bind are carefully knotted.
They are nurtured and cherished – lest they be forgotten.
They are valued as art from the Master's hand.
You seem the ties that bind belong to a very special man.

## *Watch Her Soar*

For now, we take each day as it comes.
  We rise and we fall.
We greet new challenges with faith of triumph.
We celebrate each step of progress as though it is
the greatest of blessings no matter how big or small.
We wait and watch; teach and test;
cry and cheer; and laugh and love.
Always knowing we are that much closer to the moment
that we can let her go, and watch her soar.

# Great is the Man I know as Dad

Early in my life, I realized what I had –
a man to teach me right from wrong.
Great is the man I know as Dad.
A figure I feared and whose approval I wanted to have.
Great is the man I know as Dad.
I often disturbed him early in the day –
interrupting the only quiet time he had.
Great is the man I know as Dad.
Grumbling and mumbling and wanting my way.
I didn't appreciate all that I had.
Great is the man I know as Dad.
Often, he worried as I learned to spread my wings.
Knowing the hurt the world often brings.
Seeing me stumble and fall made him sad.
Great is the man I know as Dad.
The years have gone by since I was a child –
older and wiser, and now I am glad.
For great is the man I know as Dad.
    His discipline made me strong;
    His instruction made me wise;
    His worry made me sensitive;

His dreams made me sad because
    For me was his sacrifice.
    And for me did he toil.
    I may be all grown up now,
    But I'm still his little girl.
Yes, great is the man I know as Dad.
Lord, I thank you for all the good times and the bad.
For great is the man You gave me as Dad.

## Mom – Faithful and True

M om has always been there in the good times and the bad.
She offers her full support and gives all she had.

Mom has always been faithful and true.
She put her needs aside to make life good for you.

Mom has always been protective of her own.
She let you know you weren't in this life alone.

Mom has always worked through the day and the night.
She used all her talents to help you be raised right.

Mom has always pushed you to be the best in all you did.
She was always proud to claim you as her kid.

Mom made sure we went to church
and prayed for us each day.
She also made sure we knew the value of play.

Mom encouraged us to spread our wings and fly.
She often saw us make mistakes,

and I'm sure she thought, "Why?"

Mom's life has had its share of challenges – this is true.
She faced each one with unconditional love
as only a mom can do.

Mom's also been blessed with an abundantly full life.
She's been mother, sister, brother, friend and wife.

Mom is still there for us even though we are all grown.
She patiently waits to help us –
it's the only way she's known.

Kim was born in Louisville, Kentucky.
The seventh of eight children, she grew
up in Shively. She graduated from Butler
High School, then received her degree
from Bellarmine College.
Kim currently lives in Palmyra, Indiana
with her husband, James and
her daughter, Jami.
She enjoys writing, crafting,
and spending time with
her family and friends.
She advocates for awareness
and acceptance of those with
Autism and Huntington's Disease.